Science Experiments

WITH

COLOUR

Sally Nankivell-Aston
and Dorothy Jackson

W

FRANKLIN WATTS

NEW YORK • LONDON • SYDNEY

First published in 2000 by Franklin Watts
96 Leonard Street, London EC2A 4XD

Franklin Watts Australia
14 Mars Road
Lane Cove
NSW 2066

Series editor: Rachel Cooke
Designer: Mo Choy
Picture research: Susan Mennell
Photography: Ray Moller, unless otherwise
acknowledged

A CIP catalogue record for this book
is available from the British Library.

ISBN 0 7496 3648 3

Dewey Classification 535.6

Printed in Malaysia

Acknowledgements: Cover: Steve Shott;
AKG London p.6br (Musée Condé, Chantilly);
Bruce Coleman pp.4b (Christer Fredriksson), 5bl
(Jules Cowan), 14t (Joe McDonald); Image Bank
pp.9bl (Jeff Spielman), 9br (Andy Caulfield);
Oxford Scientific Films pp.4m (Alistair Shay),
5tr, 5br (Robin Redfern), 12b (Zig Leszczynski), 29tr
(Michael Fogden), 29b (Wendy Shattil and Bob
Rozinski); Panos Pictures pp.17m (Ray Wood),
25tr (James Bedding); Science Photo Library pp. 4t
(John Mead), 10b (Vaughan Fleming), 19t (Jerry
Mason), 27t (Jon Wilson).
Thanks, too, to our models: Erin Bhogal, Perry
Christian, Bonita Crawley, Jaimé Leigh Pyle, Jordan
Oldfield, Nicholas Payne, Jennifer Quaife and
Alexander Smale

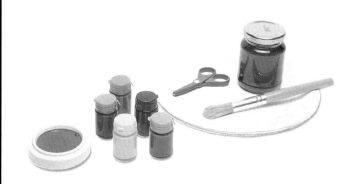

Contents

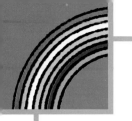

Colour all around

Look around you wherever you are and you see colours. Colours can be bright or dull, 'warm' or 'cold', blend together or contrast, they may be natural or made artificially. Look at the pictures and see how many shades of the same colour you can spot.

What is your favourite colour? Is it the same colour that your friend likes best? Discover all about your favourite colours as you do the experiments in this book.

Be amazed!

By doing the experiments in this book you can find out some amazing things about colour. You will find out about the colours of paint and light, how we see colours and how colours can be useful to us, other animals and plants. Some experiments may answer questions that you already ask about colour. Some may make you think of more!

Look closely!

Scientists always ask lots of questions and observe carefully. When you are doing experiments in this book, look closely to see what is happening and keep accurate records of your results. Don't be upset if your predictions do not always turn out to be correct as scientists (and that includes you) learn a lot from unexpected results.

Be careful!

Always make sure an adult knows that you are doing an experiment. Ask for help if you need to use sharp tools, heat things or use chemicals. Follow the step-by-step instructions carefully and remember – be a safe scientist!

Mixing paints

HAVE YOU EVER NOTICED how many different colours of paint you can buy? Each paint contains a natural or artificial pigment to give it colour. All colour pigments are actually made by mixing only two or more of three colours: red, yellow and blue. These are the primary colours of pigments. Find out more in this first experiment.

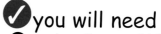

you will need
- red, yellow and blue poster paints
- large pieces of white paper
- 3 paintbrushes
- drinking straw
- 3 saucers

1 Put a small pool of paint on each saucer – one colour onto each. The paint must be runny so add water if necessary and mix in with a paintbrush. Use a separate paintbrush for each colour.

2 Use the paintbrushes to scatter drops of the three colours, each colour on a separate piece of paper. Then put drops of a second colour as shown. Don't let the drops touch each other!

In action

Today most paint pigments are made from artificial ingredients. However they used to be made from natural materials like plants, rocks and dead insects. The pigment for the blue paint in this 15th-century picture was made by crushing the semiprecious stone, lapis lazuli.

3 Use the straw to blow the paint across the paper so that the colours mix.

4 What happens when red and yellow mix? What happens when red and blue mix? What happens when yellow and blue mix? The mixed colours are called secondary colours. Put your answers on a table like the one below.

Keep thinking

How would you make a paint lighter? How could you make paint darker? How could you get different shades of green?

PRIMARY COLOURS MIXED	SECONDARY COLOUR MADE
red and yellow	
yellow and blue	
red and blue	

5 Now find out what colour you get if all three primary colours are mixed together. This is called a tertiary colour.

Don't stop there

● Drop oil-based inks (marbling inks) onto water in a tray. Swirl the colours around with a cocktail stick. What colours do you get? 'Capture' the colours by gently lowering a piece of paper on top of the water and then removing it carefully.

● Go to a DIY store and get some paint charts. How many different types of blue are there? How many different types of red are there?

Mixing light

ALTHOUGH LIGHT USUALLY looks white it is really made up of different colours. The primary colours of light are red, green and blue. They are not exactly the same as those in pigments and they don't mix in the same way. Find out how these colours of light mix in this experiment.

✓ **you will need**
- ✓ 3 torches with strong beams
- ✓ 3 colour filters (red, green and blue)
- ✓ 3 kitchen roll cardboard tubes
- ✓ sticky tape
- ✓ 2 friends

1 Fix a colour filter over the end of each cardboard tube with tape.

2 Hold a tube and shine a torch beam down the open end onto a pale coloured wall in a dark room. Ask your friends to do the same with the other two tubes. Can you see each colour on the wall?

Keep thinking

Look back to pages 6/7 to find out which of the primary colours of light are the same as the primary colours of pigments.

3 What colour do you predict you will see when the red and green lights are mixed together? Find out by making the two colours of light overlap on the wall.

4 In the same way find out what happens when red and blue lights mix, then green and blue? The resulting colours are called the secondary colours of light.

PRIMARY COLOURS MIXED	SECONDARY COLOUR MADE
red and green	
red and blue	
green and blue	

5 Record your results on a table like this one.

Don't stop there

● Find out what colour you get when all three are mixed together.

● You can split white light into its different colours using a prism. Shine a strong torch beam through a prism placed on a light piece of paper. What colours can you see on the paper?

In action

Dramatic lighting effects are achieved by mixing different coloured spotlights in theatres, at pop concerts or even on a dance floor.

Seeing colours

IMAGINE WHAT THE world would look like if you couldn't see any colours! We have special cells called cones in our eyes that let us to see in colour. There are about 7 million cones in each of your eyes!

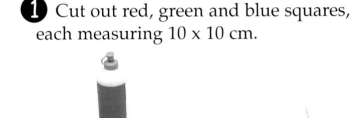

iris
retina
pupil
lens
cone

This diagram shows the different parts of the eye and a close up of some of its cones, which are found in the retina. Some cones see red, some blue and others green. Find out more in this eye-opening experiment!

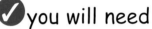

you will need
- coloured paper (red, green and blue)
- 4 pieces of white A4 card
- scissors
- pencil
- ruler
- glue

❶ Cut out red, green and blue squares, each measuring 10 x 10 cm.

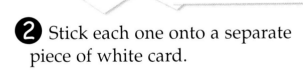

❷ Stick each one onto a separate piece of white card.

In action

This is a TV screen close up! Pictures on the screen are made up of tiny dots or stripes of green, red and blue – the primary colours of light. Looked at from a distance, these colours mix and merge to form the multicoloured picture we see.

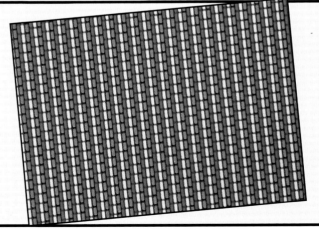

3 Now stare hard at the card with the red square for 30 seconds.

4 Then quickly look at a plain white piece of card. What do you see?

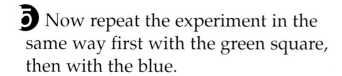

5 Now repeat the experiment in the same way first with the green square, then with the blue.

6 What shape do you see on the white piece of card each time? What colour is it? Add your results to a table like the one below.

COLOUR OF SQUARE	red	green	blue
SHAPE OF IMAGE SEEN ON WHITE CARD			
COLOUR OF IMAGE SEEN ON WHITE CARD			

Keep thinking

As you stared at a coloured square the cones that see that colour got tired so only the cones that see the other two colours were working. How does this explain what you saw when you looked at the plain white card?

Don't stop there

● Repeat the experiment with a yellow square. What colour is the image this time?

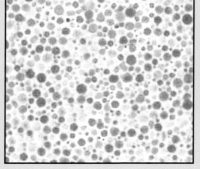

● People who are colour blind cannot see certain colours. Look at this picture. Can you see the number? Some colour-blind people would not be able to read the number picked out in shades of green.

Standing out

COLOURS ARE OFTEN USED to make things stand out and be noticed. For example, cyclists often wear bright colours so motorists can see them easily. Find out which colours stand out best in this experiment.

✓ **you will need**
- ✓ 6 thick marker pens, various colours
- ✓ 6 pieces of white card
- ✓ tape measure
- ✓ a friend

1 Draw a large exclamation mark on each piece of white card using a different coloured marker pen each time. Make sure they are all about the same size and shape to make the test fair.

2 Predict which colour can be seen from the furthest distance.

Keep thinking

Male birds are often brightly coloured so they can be seen easily. Why do you think they want to be noticed?

In action

Some animals are brightly coloured to warn other animals that they are dangerous or taste disgusting. This tree frog is poisonous. Its colour warns other animals not to eat it.

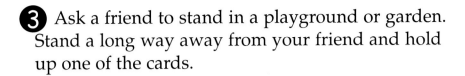

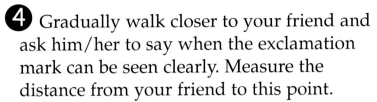

3 Ask a friend to stand in a playground or garden. Stand a long way away from your friend and hold up one of the cards.

4 Gradually walk closer to your friend and ask him/her to say when the exclamation mark can be seen clearly. Measure the distance from your friend to this point.

5 Repeat the test with the other colours and record your results in a table like this:

COLOUR OF EXCLAMATION MARK	DISTANCE IT CAN BE SEEN FROM

6 Which colour was easiest to see? Which was most difficult? Which colour would be best to use to write DANGER on a warning sign?

Don't stop there

● Cut out some exclamation marks from white paper (they must be the same size and shape). Stick each one on a different coloured piece of card or paper. Repeat the experiment to see which coloured background makes the white exclamation mark stand out most.

● Look around at signs on the roads and streets. Which colours have been used to make the signs?

Now you see me, now you don't!

ALTHOUGH SOME ANIMALS are brightly coloured to be noticed, others have dull colours to help them hide. They are camouflaged amongst the colours of their natural environment. This means that predators can hunt without being seen and prey animals are less likely to be caught. Find out more about camouflage in this experiment.

In action

Chameleons are camouflage experts! As the colours around them change, their skin colour changes to match.

you will need
- ✓ brown and black felt tip pens
- ✓ 2 hard-boiled hen eggs (brown)
- ✓ a range of natural materials collected from a park or garden
- ✓ different art/craft materials in assorted colours

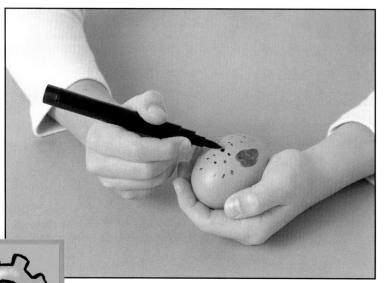

❶ First add speckles to your eggs with the felt tip pens to make them look like this quail egg.

2 Now make two nests, one using the art materials and the other using the natural materials you have collected. Use lots of bright colours for the nest made of art materials but make the natural nest roughly match the colours on the egg.

3 Place an egg in each nest and look at the nests from a short distance.

Keep thinking

Patterns help to camouflage animals because they break up the outline of the animal's body. Zebras live on wide grassy plains, tigers in shady jungle. What other animals have patterns to help them hide?

4 Which egg is easiest to see? Why is it easy to see? Which is most difficult? Why? Which nest hides the egg best? Why do you think eggs need to be well hidden?

Don't stop there

● Put the nests in a garden or nature area at school. How long does it take your friends to spot each one? Which is easiest to find? Why?

● Make flower shapes out of different colours of tissue paper. Scatter them around a garden. Which colours are easier to see and which are more difficult?

Hot or cold?

WHY DO PEOPLE OFTEN WEAR white clothes on hot summer days and black clothes during cold winter months? Do you think white clothes make you feel cooler and black clothes make you feel warmer? Find out in this experiment.

✓ **you will need**
- ✓ a small piece of black fur fabric
- ✓ a small piece of white fur fabric
- ✓ 2 thermometers
- ✓ sticky tape

1 Look at the thermometers and make a record of the temperature readings before you start the experiment. They should be the same on both.

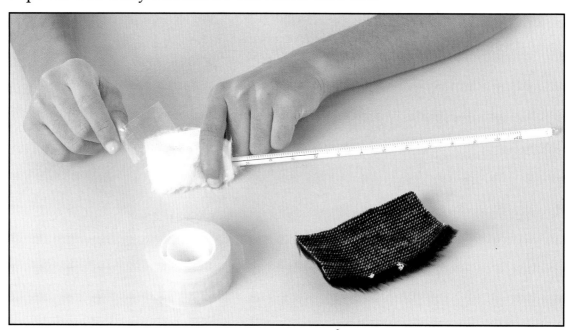

2 Wrap a small piece of white fur fabric around one of the thermometer bulbs and a black piece around the other. The pieces should be the same size and big enough to wrap around the bulb once. Hold the fabric in place with a small piece of tape.

Keep thinking

What colour clothes do you think would make you feel coolest on a hot day?

3 Put both thermometers on a sunny windowsill, with the tape underneath. Read the temperatures of each thermometer every 15 minutes for 2 hours. Make a table like this to record your results.

TIME	TEMPERATURE OF WHITE THERMOMETER	TEMPERATURE OF BLACK THERMOMETER
0 mins		
15 mins		
30 mins		
45 mins		
1 hr		
1 hr 15 mins		
1 hr 30 mins		
1 hr 45 mins		
2 hrs		

4 Which thermometer became the hottest? Did the white fabric or the black fabric let the most heat through? Some colours reflect more heat than others, while others absorb heat better. Which fabric reflected the most heat? Do you think white fabrics would keep you cooler on a hot day? Would black fabrics make you feel warmer?

In action

People who live in hot countries often wear light-coloured, loose-fitting clothes to help them keep cool. This man lives in the hot desert regions of Mali in West Africa.

Don't stop there

● Repeat the experiment using different colours of fur fabric or felt. Find out which colours absorb the most heat.

● Put a large piece of fur fabric with a black-and-white design (e.g. imitation cow's skin) in strong sunlight for about half an hour. Stroke your hand over the fabric. Can you feel a difference in temperature between the black and white areas?

A colour detective

A DETECTIVE FOUND A MYSTERIOUS, unsigned note from a criminal. She knew it had been written using one of two black marker pens: one pen belonged to suspect A and one pen belonged to suspect B. The pens were different makes and the detective knew how to find out quickly which suspect had written the note. She used a scientific process called chromatography which separates colours. Here is how the detective solved the case.

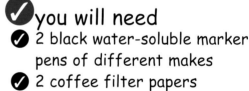

you will need
- 2 black water-soluble marker pens of different makes
- 2 coffee filter papers
- 2 drinking beakers
- dropper (pipette)
- water in a pot

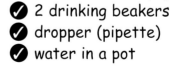

1 In the centre of each coffee filter paper make a small spot about 1 cm in diameter using one marker pen for each filter. Place a filter paper on top of each beaker.

2 Use the dropper to drop water carefully onto each coloured ink spot. Put the same number of drops on each one to make the test fair.

3 Look closely to see what happens to the colour spot from each pen as the ink dissolves in the water and spreads out.

In action

Chromatography helps scientists to study diseases, such as cancer. They use it to test tiny samples taken from the human body. There are small differences in the pattern made from a healthy sample and the one made from a sample with the disease.

Keep thinking

Look back to pages 6/7 to find out what colours are made when different coloured paints or pigments are mixed. Did this experiment show the results you expected?

4 Do both ink spots make the same pattern? What colours make up the black colour of each marker? Were you surprised?

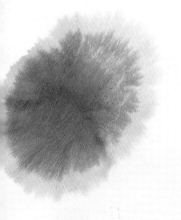

5 How could the detective use the results from this experiment to find out who had written the note?

Don't stop there

● Try repeating the experiment using markers of different colours and find out what colours each one is made from.

● Use chromatography to find out if black writing ink used in fountain pens is made of a mixture of colours. If so are they the same colours as those in black marker pen ink?

Appearing pictures

SOME CHEMICALS CHANGE from transparent to a colour in heat. Amaze your friends with this experiment and make a picture appear 'magically' on plain white paper.

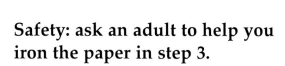

✔ **you will need**
- ✔ lemon juice in a small pot
- ✔ plain white paper
- ✔ a thin paintbrush
- ✔ a friend!

1 Use the paintbrush to draw a picture with lemon juice on the paper.

2 Leave the paper to dry so you can hardly see the picture. You have hidden your picture! Show the paper to a friend and ask him or her what they can see on the paper.

Keep thinking

What other materials can you think of that change colour when they are heated or burnt?

3 Ask an adult to iron over the back of the paper (that is, the side you did not draw on) with a hot iron.

In action

Prisoners used to use saliva or sweat to write secret messages which could be smuggled out to their friends. The messages could only be seen and read when they were heated.

4 Show your friend the paper now. What can be seen? What has changed in the heat to make your picture 'appear'?

Don't stop there

● Do you think other transparent liquids will change in the same way when they are heated? Try the experiment using lemonade and vinegar. What other liquids could you try?
● Ask an adult to light a match. Blow the flame out and look closely at the colour of the wood. How has heat affected the colour of the wood? In what other ways has the wood changed?

Colour tests

YOU CAN USE COLOUR to find out more about the foods we eat and the chemicals we use at home. Some things are acid, some are the opposite, alkaline, and some are neutral, which is in between. Find out more in this experiment.

✔ **you will need**
- ✔ 1 teaspoon each of bicarbonate of soda, lemon juice, washing-up liquid and salt, each on a separate saucer
- ✔ small fresh red cabbage
- ✔ dropper (pipette)
- ✔ small bowl
- ✔ saucepan
- ✔ sieve
- ✔ water

Safety: ask an adult for help with step 1.

1 Chop up some red cabbage leaves and put them into a saucepan with a little water. Heat the pan and boil the cabbage for a few minutes.

2 Let it cool and strain the juice into the bowl. Throw away the cabbage but keep the juice. The juice is for testing the chemicals to find out if they are acid or alkaline. We call it an indicator. What colour is your indicator? It may vary, depending on the type of saucepan you use.

In action

This is universal indicator paper, which scientists use to test for acid and alkaline. Sometimes they test for acid rain which damages plant life, buildings and stone statues.

3 Now add four drops of cabbage water to each saucer containing the kitchen chemicals.

Look closely to see the colour changes of each liquid. Record your results in a table like the one shown.

	COLOUR WHEN CABBAGE WATER IS ADDED	IS IT ACID, ALKALINE OR NEUTRAL?
bicarbonate of soda		
lemon juice		
washing-up liquid		
salt		

4 Red cabbage water is a natural indicator that can be used to tell if substances are acid or alkaline. It turns red in acids and blue/green in alkaline substances. In neutral substances that are neither acid nor alkaline its colour does not change. Can you tell which of your chemicals are acid, alkaline or neutral? Add this to your table.

Don't stop there

● Repeat the experiment to test other foods and common chemicals. You could try milk, orange juice, shower gel and sugar. BE CAREFUL! Ask an adult first in case you want to test something that is harmful. DO NOT use strong or bleach-based cleaning solutions. Record your results in a table.

● Try the experiment again with the water from boiling fresh beetroot (it needs longer cooking than cabbage). What colour changes do you get this time? Are they the same as the colours made with red cabbage water?

Dyeing for colour

WHAT COLOUR IS YOUR favourite shirt or jumper? It was probably dyed using artificial chemicals but how do you think the first dyes were made? Find out how to dye your own fabric using natural colours from everyday things in this experiment.

Safety: ask an adult for help with this experiment.

1 First predict what colour dye each of the different foods will make. Record your ideas in a table like the one shown.

2 Prepare the fabrics to be dyed by tying elastic bands tightly at intervals along each piece as shown in the picture.

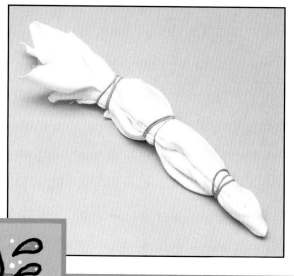

you will need
- 4 pieces of white cotton fabric, such as handkerchiefs or pieces of an old T-shirt
- onion skins from at least 2 onions
- a fresh beetroot chopped into small pieces
- red cabbage chopped up   spoon
- 3 tea bags
- 4 small bowls
- elastic bands
- saucepan
- sieve

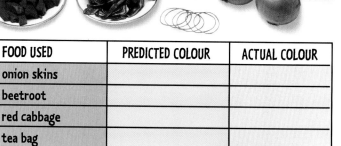

FOOD USED	PREDICTED COLOUR	ACTUAL COLOUR
onion skins		
beetroot		
red cabbage		
tea bag		

3 Now make your first dye with the onion skins. Put them into the saucepan and pour on enough water to cover them.

Ask an adult to boil up the skins until you can see that the colour from the skins has gone into the water.

4 Use the sieve to strain the coloured liquid into a bowl. This is your dye. Put a piece of fabric into the hot liquid and stir it around with a spoon.

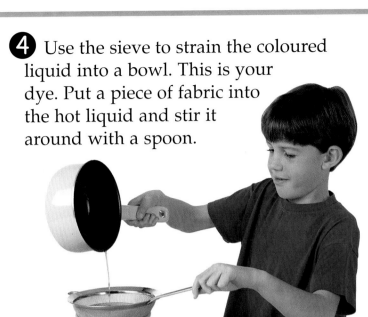

5 Make dyes with the other foods in the same way and put one piece of fabric into each bowl. Leave over night then take out the fabrics and remove the elastic bands.

Keep thinking

Some people make pictures by painting wax onto fabric then dyeing it. Then they iron the fabric between paper to remove the wax. This kind of dyeing is called batik. What effect do you think the wax has?

6 Look closely to see what has happened to the fabric. What colour has the dye from each food turned the fabric? Were your predictions correct? What has happened where the elastic was tied around the fabric? Why?

Don't stop there

● Try to make dye from other foods and plants. You could try petals from brightly coloured flowers, grass, blackberries and coffee. Predict the colour first then make the dyes to find the results.

● Repeat the experiment using different fabrics, such as wool or synthetics, to find out if all cloth absorbs colours from plants in the same way.

Going green!

WHAT COLOUR ARE THE LEAVES of most plants? Do you know why? Plants make their food (a sugar called glucose) using the energy from sunlight, water, carbon dioxide and a green-coloured chemical called chlorophyll. This process is called photosynthesis. Chlorophyll is found mostly in the leaves. Do this experiment and find out more about going green.

✔ **you will need**
- ● two similar green-leafed house-plants (NB Don't use a plant with variegated leaves)
- ● a dark cupboard
- ● labels
- ● pen

❶ Label the plants A and B. Look closely at the colour of the leaves. Make sure that the plants are well watered.

❷ Put plant A into a very dark cupboard – make sure no light can reach it. Put plant B in a light place. Leave both plants for about a week.

Leaves of plants are not always the same shade of green because they contain other pigments as well as chlorophyll. This copper beech still makes its food by photosynthesis but the green chlorophyll is masked by the 'copper' pigments.

3 Take plant A out of the cupboard and place it next to plant B. What do you notice about each plant? Do they still look the same?

4 If the plant has no energy from light it cannot make food and the leaves loose their green colour. What do you think will happen if you put plant B into the cupboard and leave plant A in the light? Test to find out.

5 Leave the plants for the same time as before and then compare them again. What do you notice now? Why do you think the plants have changed?

Keep thinking

In autumn, the leaves on many trees change colour when they die and fall off the tree. Why do you think the leaves lose their green colour?

Don't stop there

Get a plant that has red or patterned leaves. What do you think will happen this time if you repeat the experiment? Test to find out.

Fabulous flowers

Wᴴᴬᵀ ɪꜱ ʏᴏᴜʀ ꜰᴀᴠᴏᴜʀɪᴛᴇ colour? Do you think insects have favourite colours, too? Find out about why flowers have such fabulous colours in this experiment.

Note: it is better to do this experiment in spring or summer when there are plenty of insects around.

✅ **you will need**
- ✅ red, blue, green, yellow, purple and orange paint
- ✅ 7 white paper plates
- ✅ scissors
- ✅ honey

1 First turn the paper plates into 'flowers'. Cut petal shapes from around the edge as shown and paint each plate a different colour. Leave one white.

2 Put a teaspoon of honey in the centre of each plate. Place the plates in open spaces around a garden or playground on a sunny day.

Keep thinking

Look back to pages 12 and 13 to find out which colour was easiest to see when you made your signs. Is this the same colour as the flower that attracted the most insects in this experiment?

3 Watch carefully for half an hour to see how many insects and other small creatures visit each flower.

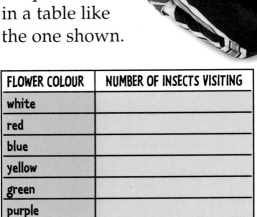

Keep a record in a table like the one shown.

FLOWER COLOUR	NUMBER OF INSECTS VISITING
white	
red	
blue	
yellow	
green	
purple	
orange	

In action

Like many insects, this hummingbird is attracted to brightly coloured flowers and feeds from the sugary nectar inside them. Some pollen from the flowers sticks to the hummingbird and is taken to the next flower it visits. This flower is now able to form seeds, so new plants can grow. This process is called pollination.

4 Which colour flower do the insects visit most? Have you seen lots of real flowers of this colour? Why is it useful to flowers if insects visit them? Which colour do insects visit least? Do you see many flowers of this colour? If not, why not?

Don't stop there

● In an area of wild flowers find out the most common flower colour. Is it the same colour that you found insects visited most?

● Repeat the experiment, but this time keep a record of the type of insects that visit the flowers as well. Do different types of insect prefer different colours?

Glossary

This glossary gives the meaning of each word as it is used in this book.

Acid A chemical that is acid turns indicators red.

Acid rain Acidic pollution from factories and car exhausts carried in the air can dissolve in the water held in clouds. This water then falls as acid rain.

Alkaline A chemical that is alkaline turns indicators blue/green.

Batik A method of producing patterned fabrics using wax to stop dye(s) colouring parts of the fabric.

Camouflage Colourings or patterns to make an animal, person, vehicle or another object difficult to see in its surroundings.

Carbon dioxide A gas in the air that plants use to make food in the process of photosynthesis.

Cell Very small parts of all living things. Cells are sometimes called the building blocks of life.

Chlorophyll The green chemical in plants, that enables them to make food using energy from sunlight, carbon dioxide from the air and water from the ground in a process called photosynthesis.

Chromatography A technique used to separate a mixture of different chemicals, such as pigments, into its different parts.

Colour blind People who are colour blind are unable to see certain colours.

Colour filter A transparent piece of coloured material that allows only light of that colour to pass through it.

Cones Cells in the retina of the eye that enable us to see things in colour.

Diameter The straight line from one edge of a circle to the other passing through its centre.

Dye To dye something is to change its colour by soaking it in a specially coloured liquid. The liquid is also called a dye.

Energy People, plants and animals need energy to live. Machines need energy to work. Energy comes from lots of different sources. Burning petrol gives a car its energy. Food gives us our energy.

Experiment A fair test done to find out more about something or to answer a question. Sometimes called an investigation.

Fair test A scientific test to find an accurate result. To keep the test fair, when you are experimenting, only one part (variable) must be changed and all the other parts (variables) must stay the same.

Filter paper Absorbent paper with very fine holes in it.

Glucose A type of sugar.

Indicator A substance used to find out, or indicate, if a chemical is acid or alkaline.

Iris The coloured part of the eye that surrounds the pupil.

Lapis lazuli A semiprecious, blue mineral that used to be used to make a bright blue pigment for paints. Today, lapis lazuli is more often used in jewellery.

Lens In an eye, the lens focuses the light that enters through the pupil to form a clear image on the retina.

Nectar A sweet liquid made in the flowers of some plants to attract insects and other animals to visit them to help the process of pollination.

Neutral A chemical that is neutral is neither acid nor alkaline. Pure water is neutral.

Photosynthesis The process by which plants use energy from the sun and chlorophyll to make their food.

Pigment A material used to colour paints, inks or dyes.

Pollen Very small grains from the male part of a flower.

Pollination The process by which pollen is transferred from the male part of a flower to a female part to make seeds from which new plants can grow.

Predators Animals that hunt and eat other animals for food.

Predict To guess what will happen in an experiment before doing it.

Prey Animals that are hunted and eaten by other animals for food.

Primary colours of light The three colours of light, red, green and blue, which can be mixed together to create all other light colours.

Primary colours of pigment The three pigment colours, red, blue and yellow, which can be mixed together to create all other colours.

Prism A solid piece of transparent glass or plastic (often looking like a pyramid) that can be used to split white light into its colours.

Pupil A small hole in the iris that lets light into the eye.

Quail A small, short-tailed bird that is a member of the partridge family.

Result(s) The outcome of an experiment.

Retina The back of the inside of the eye made up of light-sensitive cells.

Saliva The liquid in your mouth that helps you to digest and swallow your food.

Secondary colour The colour made when two primary colours mix.

Temperature How hot or cold something is. Temperature is measured in degrees Celsius or Fahrenheit.

Tertiary colour The colour made when three primary colours mix.

Thermometer An instrument to measure temperature.

Transparent Completely see-through.

Universal indicator paper Paper that contains an indicator so that it changes colour when dipped in something that is acid or alkaline. Litmus paper is also used for this.

Index

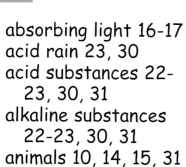